The Only Son

By Trevor Wilson

Illustrated by Mario Capaldi

✦ Dominie Press, Inc.

Publisher: Raymond Yuen
Project Editor: John S. F. Graham
Editor: Bob Rowland
Designer: Greg DiGenti
Illustrator: Mario Capaldi

Published by:

🏮 **Dominie Press, Inc.**

1949 Kellogg Avenue
Carlsbad, California 92008 USA

www.dominie.com

1-800-232-4570

Paperback ISBN 0-7685-1819-9
Printed in Singapore by PH Productions Pte Ltd
1 2 3 4 5 6 PH 05 04 03

Table of Contents

Chapter One
A Wonderful Offer

A long time ago, a farmer and his wife lived near a village called Clearwater. Their baby boy had golden hair like his father's. He grew up to be a bright young man.

"We have been blessed," the farmer

and his wife told each other. "We have a son to be proud of."

One day, a merchant passed through Clearwater and saw the boy, who was helping the farmer in his fields. The merchant was looking for a young man to work in his warehouse, so he went up to the farmer.

"How can we help you, sir?" asked the farmer.

"If you let this boy come and work for me," said the merchant, "I will teach him to become a trader."

The farmer looked at his wife, who had turned pale. "That's... That's a wonderful offer, sir, but he's our only son."

"I know how you feel," said the merchant. "But wouldn't you like to give him the chance of a lifetime? As a rich man, he can come back and look after

you in your old age."

The farmer and his wife had some doubts, but the merchant talked them into letting their only son leave for the big city.

"Are you sure you don't need me?" asked the son.

"You go, my boy," said his father. "This is a wonderful chance for you."

With tears in her eyes, the boy's mother gave him a hug. "Work hard and let us know how you are doing," she said.

Chapter Two
As Bald as an Egg

True to his word, the merchant trained the boy to be a good trader. All went well until a fire in the city destroyed the merchant's warehouse. Without insurance, the merchant was ruined.

"You'd better go back to your parents," he said.

But the son had his heart set on becoming successful, and he didn't want to go home as poor as he had left. He spent the next few weeks begging for scraps of food and small change.

Whenever he had enough pennies for paper and postage, he sent letters to his parents. The letters were filled with tales the boy made up about being a hard-working young man in the city.

Little did his parents know that their only son had become sick through lack of food. His golden hair had fallen out, and his head was as bald as an egg.

Still too proud to admit that he was a beggar, the son signed someone else's name on his next letter home.

Chapter Three
Come in and Rest

When the boy's parents read the letter, they were overcome with grief.

"Oh, my poor boy!" wept his mother. His father, too, was shaken.

The message told them that their only son had been lost at sea.

Years passed by, and the boy became too sick and weary to continue begging in the streets. He decided there was only one place he could go. By the time he set off for home, he had grown a long beard, the same color as his lost hair. After his illness, he was sure that his parents wouldn't recognize him.

When he reached the farm, he knocked on the door.

"Have you any work for a poor man?" he asked, surprised to see how much his father had aged.

"I'm sorry," said the old man. "Our farm isn't big enough to hire help, but you look weary. Come in and rest."

"Thank you," said the son. He followed his father into the kitchen.

He was surprised to see that his mother's dark hair was now as white as

a summer cloud.

She laid out some bread and cheese and a tumbler of tea.

"Have you come far?" she asked.

"Yes, I have walked for many days," said the son.

Though they couldn't put their finger on it, there was something about this stranger that the old couple liked.

"I said we didn't have any work for you," said his father, "but maybe I could use some help."

The son bowed his head. "Thank you for your kindness, sir. I'll do anything at all."

"Here are some clean clothes for you," said his mother. "They belonged to our only son, who was lost at sea."

"I'm very sorry," said the son, taking his own clothes.

He dearly wanted to tell his parents the truth, but pride is as strong as iron. "I'll tell them later," he told himself.

Chapter Four
Only a Miracle

The son kept telling himself he would tell his parents the truth, but he never did. Time slipped by, and gradually the farmer allowed his helper to take over running the farm. All went well until the farmer's wife fell ill. Slowly, she became worse.

"There is nothing more I can do," said the village doctor. "Only a miracle can save her now."

This came as a terrible blow to the old man. The son didn't know what to do. "Why didn't I tell them from the start?" he lamented to himself.

Then he recalled the doctor's words, *Only a miracle can save her now.* That gave him an idea. One day, he went into town and returned, shaking his head.

"I've just got some bad news," he said. "I'm sorry to leave you at such a time, but I must go back home."

His father turned pale.

"Must you? We have come to think of you as one of our own. You have been like a son to us. This will come as a great blow to my wife."

"I'm sorry," said the son, "but my own mother is ill, and I must go to her."

"Of course you must," said his father.

So the son left with two gold coins that his father pressed into his hand.

When the old man told his wife that their helper had left, she turned her face to the wall.

"He was a fine young man," she whispered. "You will miss him."

Chapter Five
A Wig

The son hurried to a barber in the next town.

"Can you shave off my beard and make my whiskers into a wig?"

"Yes," said the barber, and in no time the beard was a heap of hair on the

son's lap.

That night he slept badly, afraid that he wouldn't get back to Clearwater in time.

The next morning, when he put on the wig and looked in the mirror, his old self stared back at him.

"Heaven help me if I'm too late," he whispered as he hurried home.

When he knocked on the cottage door, he heard his father's shuffling steps.

"Father!" he cried as the door opened. "Father! I'm home!"

"My son," murmured the old man, with tears in his eyes. Then he shook his head.

"What is wrong?" asked the son, afraid for the worst.

Chapter Six
Like Brothers

"**Y**our mother is very ill," said his father. "She has just a day or two left. You must go to her at once."

From the moment the son returned, his mother miraculously began to get better. Soon she was able to sit up.

"We thought you had drowned at sea," she said.

"That was a mistake," said the son, promising himself to tell them the whole story as soon as his mother was better.

"A young man who'd fallen on hard times came by and was like a son to us," said his father. "But not long before you arrived home, he had to leave. We're hoping he'll return one day. You two would get along like brothers."

"I don't think he will," said the son, falling silent and hanging his head. He looked into the eyes of his parents and saw how much the other young man— himself—had meant to them.

Then he took a big breath and told them the truth.